Weird & Wonderful Travels: The World's Weirdest Museums

Weird & Wonderful Travels: The World's Weirdest Museums

Terrance Zepke

Safari Publishing

Copyright © 2019 by Terrance Zepke

All rights reserved. No part of this book shall be reproduced or transmitted in any form or by any means, electronic, mechanical, magnetic, and photographic including photocopying, recording or by any information storage and retrieval system, without prior written permission of the publisher. No patent liability is assumed with respect to the use of the information contained herein. Although every precaution has been taken in the preparation of this book, the publisher and author assume no responsibility for errors or omissions. Neither is any liability assumed for damages resulting from the use of the information contained herein.

Safari Publishing

All queries should be directed to www.safaripublishing.net.

For more about this author, visit www.terrancezepke.com.

Library of Congress Cataloging-in-Publication Data

Zepke, Terrance

Weird & Wonderful Travels: The World's Weirdest Museums/ Terrance Zepke p. cm.

The World's Weirdest Museums

ISBN: 9781942738695

1. U.S. Museums. 2. World Museums. 3. Strange Tourist Attractions. 4. Travel-America. 5. Travel-World. 6. Family Travel. 7. Oddities-Travel. 8. Nonfiction-Travel. 9. Special Interest Travel. I. Title.

First edition

10 9 8 7 6 5 4 3 2 1

CONTENTS

Introduction, 7

Museums

    Cancun Underwater Museum of Art, 11
    Paris Sewer Museum, 17
    Paris Catacombs, 21
    Museum of Bad Art, 28
    Iceland Phallological Museum, 32
    Museum of Salt & Pepper Shakers, 35
    Museum of Cryptozoology, 40
    International Clown Hall of Fame, 44
    Ripley's Believe It or Not Odditorium, 47
    Siriraj Medical Museum, 50
    Kunstkamera Museum, 54
    American Museum of the House Cat, 57
    International Spy Museum, 61
    Canadian Potato Museum, 66
    Mutter Museum, 72
    National Museum of Funeral History, 75
    New Orleans Historic Voodoo Museum, 80
    Museum of Death, 83
    Museum of Clean, 87
    Vienna Undertakers' Museum, 91
    Sulabh International Museum of Toilets, 96

The World's Weirdest Museums

Museum of Icelandic Sorcery & Witchcraft, 100
Museum of Sex, 103
Mummy Museum, 106
Torture Museum, 110
British Lawnmower Museum, 113
Vent Haven Ventriloquist Museum, 118
Avanos Hair Museum, 122
Cupnoodles Museum, 126
Meguro Parasitological Museum, 130
Kansas Barbed Wire Museum, 133
Museum of Broken Relationships, 141
Bunny Museum, 145
International UFO Museum, 148
Condom Museum, 152
Hash, Marihuana & Hemp Museum, 155
Dog Collar Museum, 159

More Museums, 163

TZ Titles, 169

Sneak Peak, 182

Index, 192

Introduction

I love weird stuff and you must too if you're reading this book. I tend to lose all track of time exploring quirky attractions, like these weird museums. You better believe that I loved every minute I spent working on this book. After a great deal of research, I have compiled this list of the weirdest museums in the world—and believe me there are some you cannot even imagine!

These are "must visit" places for travelers who like to go off the beaten path or for armchair travelers. I enjoy reading about these kinds of places. I always make a note in case I get a chance to visit someday. Sometimes, I know I will never get to a certain place, but I enjoyed learning about it anyway.

Did you know there is a museum devoted to dummies? (My favorite dummy is Slappy from R.L. Stein's *Goosebump* series, but the most famous is probably Howdy Doody). Did you know there is a mummy museum (with real excavated mummies, not fake Hollywood mummies)? Did you know there are museums devoted exclusively to condoms and penium?

The World's Weirdest Museums

Did you know there is a dog collar museum? There is even a museum devoted to the history of barbed wire. I kid you not! In fact, collecting barbed wire is a popular hobby and the museum is popular too. Lovesick people from around the world have sent items for display in the Museum of Broken Relationships. And we're talking some strange contributions! Are you into Bigfoot (Yeti)? There's a museum for that too.

If you're an art lover, you may find the Museum of Bad Art to be an interesting place to visit. It is devoted to artwork that everyone can agree is just plain bad. The UFO Museum & Research Center is acclaimed for its research on extraterrestrial life and educational exhibits. A visit to the Salt & Pepper Shaker Museum is a fun way to spend an hour or so if you're in the area. The Torture Museum is definitely not for the faint at heart. Almost everyone, especially kids, will love the Ripley's Believe It or Not Odditorium. It is thousands of square feet of oddities displayed in amazing exhibits. Speaking of odd, the Icelandic Sorcery & Witchcraft Museum is a weird but wonderful place.

I learned a lot while researching this book. First and foremost, I discovered there is a museum for every interest and in every corner of the world. Also, I consider myself a seasoned traveler, but I had never heard of most of these museums. Certainly, I had no idea the public had such a fascination with death and food! There are museums devoted to about every kind of food you can imagine, from ramen noodles to Idaho potatoes. The same is true with death. There is a National Museum of Funeral History, Paris Catacombs, Museum of Death, and the Vienna Undertakers' Museum. Did you know a reusable coffin was invented?

In the interest of full disclosure, I must admit there were a few museums I did not visit, such as the parasite, toilet, and hair museums.

At the end of each chapter, there is detailed visitor information, including accessibility, tourist tips, and more. I have included photos and virtual tour links when available.

The World's Weirdest Museums

To be honest, I think some of these museums are ridiculous but I think many of them are pretty cool, such as the Paris Catacombs, UFO Museum, Spy Museum, and MUSA Underwater Museum of Art. So read on to see what you think…

P.S. This is the first book in my new series, *WEIRD & WONDERFUL TRAVELS*. I hope you will join me on my journey to discover the most offbeat places worldwide. If you enjoy this fun reference, be sure to be on the lookout for the next book in this series. In the meantime, you may want to check out my *QUIRKY TRAVEL* and *SPOOKIEST* series. There is a list of all my titles in the back of this book.

Cancun Underwater Museum of Art

Location: Cancun, Mexico

The World's Weirdest Museums

Cancun Underwater Museum of Art (MUSA, Museo Subacuático de Arte) is my choice for the weirdest and most wonderful museum because of its location and exhibits. You don't walk around this art museum. You must get wet to see all its amazing art exhibits up close! The museum was the vision of Cancun National Marine Park director, Jaime Gonzalez Canto. Established in 2009, Musa now has a total of 500 massive sculptures. Most of these were created by British sculptor Jason deCaires Taylor and five Mexican sculptors (https://musamexico.org/meet-the-artists-of-musa/).

But don't worry about the impact this might have on sea life because the museum is eco-friendly. All sculptures are fixed to the seabed and made from specialized materials that actually promote coral life. They are created above ground and cleaned before being taken underwater so they do not have any chemicals on them that may harm the water, animals, or reef. Some weigh more than 200 tons. To place the statues on the ocean floor, Taylor had a special lift made for the statues so none would be damaged during the move. A forty-ton crane was placed on a commercial ferry in order to lower the sculptures. Some are so heavy that they had to be lifted into the water using lift bags.

Since the statues were made with pH-neutral cement; coral, seaweed, and algae are able to form better than on an old, sunken ship. The statues have holes in them, which allow marine wildlife to colonize and feed off the coral. As the coral reefs increase, so will marine life.

The World's Weirdest Museums

This is one of the largest and most ambitious underwater artificial art attractions in the world. The museum is meant to promote conservation, but it is also great for tourism.

This underwater museum draws more than 200,000 visitors annually. The museum is divided into three galleries offering three different ways to explore: Salon Manchones, Salon Nizuc, and Salon Punta Sam. Salon Manchones (Isla Mujeres) is best explored by scuba divers since it is eight meters down, while Salon Nizuc and Punta Sam (Cancun) are intended for snorkelers with a depth of just four meters.

If you are not a certified diver, you can take a 90-minute course which allows you to join a beginner's diving tour. Please note that you cannot see all three sites (galleries) in one dive. In addition to snorkeling and diving, you can see part of the museum by glass bottom boat if you don't like to get wet. The cost is dependent on which option you choose and what company you use. http://musamexico.org/

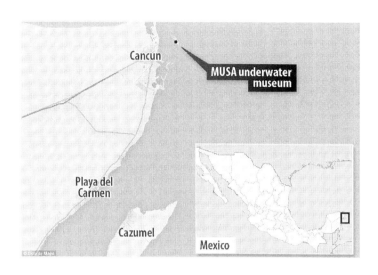

VISITOR TIPS: Use eco-friendly sunscreen if going in the water. You are permitted to swim all around the exhibits but are asked not to touch them. If you prone to motion sickness/seasickness, be sure to take a prescription or holistic remedy, such as ginger tablets or acupuncture wristbands. MUSA is located near the Manchones Reef, in the Cancun National Marine Park. There are lots of water activities available and you can also swim with dolphins in Cancun. Check out the MUSA Visitor's Center at Kukulkan Plaza where you can see replicas of the submerged statues in their original state before you visit or in lieu of visiting if you suffer motion sickness.

The World's Weirdest Museums

FYI: There are plans to ultimately expand to ten galleries featuring approximately 1,200 sculptures!

Paris Sewer Museum

Location: Paris, France

The World's Weirdest Museums

Paris Sewer Museum (Musée des Égouts de Paris), is dedicated to the sewer system of Paris. That's right. *Sewage.* But even though we are talking about sewage, tours of the sewage system have been wildly popular since the 1800s. This underground museum shares the history of Paris sewage from the late 14th century to the present. The role of sewer workers and methods of water treatment are also chronicled.

These tunnels, which extend nearly 1,500 miles underneath the city's streets, highlight the engineering genius of Eugene Belgrand. The corridors are all named after statesmen or engineers who contributed to the creation or improvement of the Paris Sewers.

The tour begins in the Galerie Hugues Aubriot corridor. Aubriot was a Provost of Paris and he commissioned Paris' first vaulted sewer in the late 14th century.

VISITOR TIPS: The tour takes about an hour and ends in the museum's gift shop. The outside entrance is well posted but watch for it because many people miss it since it is located in a small kiosk. Wear comfortable shoes and bring a sweater if you tend to get cold easily. It is appropriate for all ages. In fact, children typically love the tour. Admission is free for ages five and under. The galleries are safe with footbridges that are secured with grills. There is an acrid odor that most people get used to fairly quickly, but may be an issue for those with respiratory problems. The Paris Sewer Museum is located on Quai d'Orsay by the Pont de l'Alma and is

The World's Weirdest Museums

open Sat-Wed, but is closed for renovations until sometime in 2020.

https://en.parisinfo.com/paris-museum-monument/71499/Musee-des-egouts-de-Paris

FYI: The Paris sewer system has been referenced in great works of literature, including Victor Hugo's *Les Misérables* and Gaston Leroux's *Phantom of the Opera*.

Paris Catacombs

Location: Paris, France

The World's Weirdest Museums

Another weird museum worth seeing while in Paris is the Paris Catacombs, which is one of fourteen museums in the Paris Museum system. Dubbed the "World's Largest Grave," the catacombs are underground ossuaries containing the remains of more than six million people.

In the late eighteenth century, the dead were buried in cemeteries, covered, and a new layer for burials would be created. Areas would fill up rather quickly. Naturally, this led to sanitation concerns since the primary source of water in Paris was wells. Organic matter from the decaying corpses seeped into the ground, creating sanitation issues for city residents.

The solution chosen by city officials was to move the remains to an abandoned mine outside the city. From 1786 – 1788, bones were transported nightly by covered wagon to the catacombs.

The site was consecrated as the "Paris Municipal Ossuary" on April 7, 1786. Eventually, The Ossuary came to be known as the "Catacombs", in reference to the Roman catacombs, which had fascinated the public since their discovery.

Starting in 1809, the Catacombs were opened to the public by appointment only. As word spread about the underground cemetery, it grew in popularity as a tourist attraction. It opened for public tours in 1874.

The World's Weirdest Museums

The Paris Catacombs are a massive, 200 mile-long maze filled with twisting alleyways, old nuclear bunkers, bone-filled ossuaries, and much more.

Near one of the main entranceways to the catacombs is a place that is called "The Beach" because of a beautiful wall painting featuring a wave. Close to this, a surprising figure lurks in the dark, waiting to greet curious visitors.

Interesting Facts…

The tomb of the Val-de-Grâce hospital doorkeeper, Philibert Aspairt, lost in the catacombs during 1793 and found eleven years later, is located in the catacombs on the spot where his body was found.

During World War II, Parisian members of the French Resistance used the tunnel system.

The Nazis established an underground bunker.

During 2004, police discovered a movie theater in one of the caverns. It was equipped with a giant cinema screen, seats for the audience, projection equipment, film reels of recent thrillers and film noir classics, a fully stocked bar, and a complete restaurant with tables and chairs. The source of its electrical power and the identity of those responsible remain unknown. It has long been rumored that there are people living deep in the Catacombs where authorities never go. There are supposedly apartments and party rooms.

Ghost Adventures featured a special episode entitled "NetherWorld: Paris Catacombs".

The film *As Above, So Below*, released in 2014, was the first production that secured permission from the French government to film in the catacombs. They aimed to use no alterations to the environment with the exception of a piano and a car which were hauled into the catacombs and set on fire.

The World's Weirdest Museums

During 2015, Airbnb paid €350,000 as part of a publicity stunt offering customers the chance to stay overnight in the Catacombs.

In 2017, two teenagers were lost in the Paris catacombs for three days.

Only 1.1 miles of tunnels are open to the public. The entrance gates are locked every night, but some groups still find ways to access the tunnels to hold raging parties.

A couple of years ago, clever thieves broke into the wine cellar of a luxury apartment using the catacombs to gain access to the cellar and stole 300 bottles of fine wine valued at more than €250,000 of wine. They used the 150-mile tunnel system to escape.

VISITOR TIPS: The tour takes about one hour. For the proper preservation of the site and for safety reasons, the number of visitors at one time is limited to 200. It is not wheelchair accessible. There are 131 steps to go down and 112 steps to climb up. This tour is not recommended for pregnant women, cardiac patients, and children under ten years old. Children under fourteen must be accompanied by an adult. No food, beverages, animals, or touching any part of the catacombs is permitted. The average temperature is 57°F (14°C), but it can be very humid.

http://catacombes.paris.fr/en

Museum of Bad Art

Location: Somerville, Massachusetts

Museum of Bad Art (MOBA) features over 600 "bad"

works of art.

This is not me being overly critical. This is a fact. The museum prides itself on only displaying art that no one else will!

"MOBA is the world's only museum dedicated to the collection, preservation, exhibition and celebration of bad art in all its forms."

If you can't make it to the only museum in the world that celebrates bad artists, be sure to take their online tour of museum that includes Jerez the Clown.

You may well wonder how such a museum came into existence. The idea was born when Scott Wilson

The World's Weirdest Museums

found 'Lucy in the Field with Flowers', in the garbage. Wilson found the painting at the curb between two trash cans waiting to be hauled away by the city garbage service. He showed the artwork to a friend, Jerry Reilly, who asked if he could have it. Wilson gladly gave 'Lucy' to him.

Wilson, who was an antique dealer, continued to find ugly pieces of art that he shared with Reilly. Meanwhile, Reilly and his wife were displaying these pieces in their home to friends and neighbors. They regularly held art receptions in their basement until they outgrew their venue.

The Museum of Bad Art was moved to the lower level of the Dedham Community Theatre before relocating again to its current location. Since that time, the collection has grown to more than 700 pieces with roughly three dozen on display at any given time. 'Lucy in the Field with Flowers' remains the signature piece of the Museum of Bad Art (pictured here).

VISITOR TIPS: Admission is free with the purchase of a movie ticket or by requesting a free pass at info@museumofbadart.org. Somerville Theater, 55 Davis Square, Somerville, Massachussetts 02144. Somerville is five miles northwest of Boston.
http://www.museumofbadart.org/

The World's Weirdest Museums

Iceland Phallological Museum

Location: Reykjavik, Iceland

Iceland Phallological Museum is a seriously strange and highly unique museum. It is the only place in the world (to my knowledge and my greatest hope) that displays phallic specimens. Their collection includes 200 penises and penile parts belonging to nearly all the land and sea mammals that can be found in Iceland, including humans. I think the best section of the museum is the Folklore gallery.

If all of this is not enough, there is phallic art,

The World's Weirdest Museums

including a tree trunk carved to look like a phallus and a lampshade made from bull testicles!

In case you're wondering who would be interested, more than one hundred articles have been written and published in twenty-six countries worldwide about this odd museum. The museum was founded by a former teacher and historian, Sigurður Hjartarson.

VISITOR TIPS: This is a popular attraction. Children are welcome and ages 12 and under get free admission. Admission is discounted for seniors and the disabled. Open daily Monday – Saturday. Laugavegur 116, 105 Reykjavík, (Iceland). http://phallus.is/en/

Museum of Salt & Pepper Shakers

Location: Gatlinburg, Tennessee

The World's Weirdest Museums

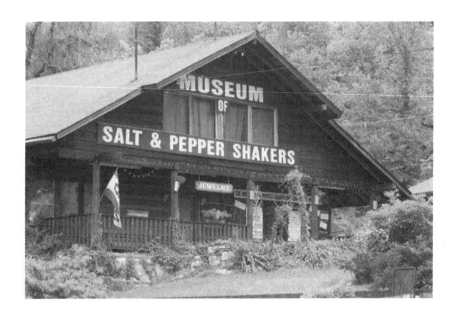

Salt and Pepper Shaker Museum boasts the world's biggest collection with more than 22,000 salt and pepper shaker sets. You can't even imagine all the designs! *Seriously!* The designs include the Beatles, Mt. Rushmore, hundreds of animals and foods, witches, and much more.

Andrea Ludden and her family moved to Cosby, Tennessee to open a museum to exhibit her vast salt and pepper shaker collection. In three short years, Ludden's collection had grown so extensive that the family had to move to bigger digs. They relocated to Gatlinburg, which is a big tourist destination and a quirky mountain community where such a museum would fit right in.

Andrea Ludden is a Belgium, trained archaeologist. As such, she appreciates the history and creativity of each and every one of her shakers. She has lovingly and carefully cultivated the display space to best showcase her exhibits. There is a gift shop where you can buy a duplicate set of your favorite shaker set.

The World's Weirdest Museums

This is the question asked most often by museum visitors:

Which Shaker has the most (or least) amount of holes - salt or pepper?

It depends! The number of holes in salt and pepper shakers varies by culture, health and taste. Here in the US excessive salt is considered bad for you, so the salt shaker is the one with the fewer holes, but in parts of Europe it's the other way around. It also has to do with availability – in some places salt was rare and prized, whereas in Europe it was difficult to get your hands on Pepper since it's a spice from the Orient (very exotic) which was used to spice up meat that was past its prime. Another factor is the size of the grains – some salts are quite coarse while others are very fine - and pepper can be ground or it can be cracked, which many cooks prefer. So, what will pour better? Exceptions abound - you can have 1, 2, 3 or more holes in a shaker, and they go from tiny holes to huge ones.
*This information was taken from the museum's website.

VISITOR TIPS: Open daily from 10 a.m. – 2 p.m. Children 12 and younger are free. 461 Brookside Village Way (Winery Square) Gatlinburg, Tennessee 37738 (U.S.).
http://thesaltandpeppershakermuseum.com/

Click here to see pictures or access a virtual tour of the museum, http://thesaltandpeppershakermuseum.com/Museum-Pictures.

International Cryptozoology Museum

Location: Portland, Maine

International Cryptozoology Museum features exhibits pertaining to all things cryptozoology. So just what exactly is cryptozoology? The word *cryptozoology* means literally the "study of hidden animals", those which some people believe are out there but science has yet to officially acknowledge, as in Bigfoot and the Loch Ness Monster. These mysterious creatures are known as *cryptids* and cryptozoologists are the ones who study them.

Loren Coleman opened the museum in 2003. Since that time it has grown so much that it has upsized three times. Currently, the museum has more than 10,000 items of evidence and interest on display. Some of the items include hair samples of Abominable Snowmen, Bigfoot, Yowie, and Orang Pendek. Also, fecal matter reportedly from a small Yeti that was collected by the Tom Slick-F. Kirk Johnson Snowman Expedition, and a footprint cast taken in 2001, during an alleged Thylacine encounter, are among the many items housed here.

The World's Weirdest Museums

The first item acquired for the museum was the guidebook used for a Yeti Himalaya expedition and there are also props from Hollywood movies that feature cryptids, such as *The Mothman Prophecies*. In addition to the cryptozoological exhibits, there is featured artwork on display.

VISITOR TIPS: Reduced rates for seniors and children. Hours vary seasonally. There are online and on-site gift shops. 11 Avon St., Portland, Maine (U.S.). <http://cryptozoologymuseum.com/>

International Clown Hall of Fame

Location: Baraboo, Wisconsin

"Clowning is a rare art form, with a heritage that transcends history. The role of the clown exists in every culture, every country, and in every walk of life."
-excerpt from ICHOF website

International Clown Hall of Fame & Research Center is one creepy place. While it is meant to be a tribute to clowns everywhere, it is also a freaky place if clowns aren't your thing. In addition to exhibits about famous clowns (and their bizarre scrapbooks), there are many clown artifacts.

The World's Weirdest Museums

VISITOR TIPS: Hours vary seasonally. Reduced rates for children under 12. 102 4th Avenue, Baraboo, Wisconsin 53913. Do not confuse this museum with the Ringling Brothers Circus Museum in Sarasota, Florida. http://www.theclownmuseum.com/

Ripley's Believe It or Not Odditorium

Location: Gatlinburg, Tennessee

The World's Weirdest Museums

Ripley's Believe It or Not Odditorium is nearly 13,000-square-feet of oddities you have to see to believe. It includes 3 floors of 16 themed galleries with 500+ artifacts and exhibits. My favorite area is the Amazonian Jungle Gallery.

Visitors will see a 19th century vampire killing kit, authentic shrunken heads (huh?), a Harry Potter Hogwarts replica made entirely out of matchsticks, and freaky two-headed animals—just to name a few!

For good luck, be sure to ring the wishing bell before stepping inside the attraction.

VISITOR TIPS: The museum is open every day year-round, even on holidays. Rates are discounted for children. 800 Parkway, Gatlinburg, TN 37738. www.ripleys.com/gatlinburg

Note: Other Ripley's Gatlinburg attractions include Haunted Adventure, Mirror Maze, and 5D Moving Theater. There are Ripley's Museums in many other locations, including Key West, Branson, and Myrtle Beach.

```
WEIRD FACT: The string on boxes of
    animal crackers was originally
placed there so the container could
   be hung from a Christmas tree.
```

The World's Weirdest Museums

Siriraj Medical Museum

Location: Bangkok, Thailand

Siriraj Medical Museum, dubbed the Museum of Death, is not a place for the squeamish. It contains skeletons, skulls, brains, and mutilated limbs. One of the most gruesome exhibits is the mummified body of Si Ouey, a serial killer in the 1950s who murdered many children and then ate the mutilated remains. He became known as a Thai bogeyman.

Founded in 1888, this is Bangkok's oldest hospital and medical school. It was established by King Rama V and it is still the place where the King of Thailand is treated when ill. And it is a fascinating place to visit for doctors,

The World's Weirdest Museums

medical students, and those intrigued by freaky things. The museum is rumored to be haunted. If you visit, you will probably see candy placed near exhibits featuring children. This is meant as an offering for the young spirits.

This museum consists of five small medical museums: Ellis Pathological Museum (chronicles the evolution of medicine), Congdon Anatomical Museum (2,000 specimens pertaining to human anatomy), Sood Sangvichien Prehistoric Museum and Laboratory (evolution of life forms dating back to prehistoric civilization), Parasitology Museum (collection of parasites), and Songkran Niyomsane Forensic Medicine Museum (Museum of Death; focuses on forensic science).

While three of them are door to door to each other, the remaining two are a short walk away in a different building. Once you pay your entry fee you can wander freely in all five different museums with its different themes and topics. All museums can easily be visited in one day, but if short on time focus on the

Songkran Niyomsane Forensic Medicine Museum and the Congdon Anatomical Museum.

VISITOR TIPS: Not appropriate for small children or the faint at heart as it is quite gruesome. Open daily except Tuesdays and holidays. Siriraj Hospital, 2, Wang Lang Road, Siriraj, Bangkok Noi, Bangkok, Thailand 10700. http://www.sirirajmuseum.com/siriraj-medical-museum-en.html

The World's Weirdest Museums

Kunstkamera Museum

Location: St. Petersburg, Russia

Kunstkamera was the first museum to open in Russia. It began in 1727 with Peter the Great's collection of curiosities and grew into a collection of roughly two million freaky objects. However, it was never Peter the Great's intention to establish a museum for the macabre. He was attempting to modernize Russia.

At that time, there was a lot of superstition surrounding death and disease. He wanted to show that disease and malformities are simply quirks of nature and not the work of demons or monsters. He went so far as to order that bodies of all deformed infants be remanded to

The World's Weirdest Museums

the museum. Peter the Great enticed Russian citizens to visit the museum by offering visitors free alcoholic drinks!

It is still unclear to me how a museum exhibiting deformed fetuses, a decapitated head, and creatures with extra limbs accomplishes that goal.

While it is now known as the Peter the Great Museum of Anthropology and Ethnography, it continues to house strange objects, including a prominent collection on Siberian shamanism.

VISITOR TIPS: There is a reduced admission fee for children and seniors. Closed Mondays, holidays, and the last Tuesday of every month. Take a virtual tour at http://tour.kunstkamera.ru/#1241881728. It is located on the Universitetskaya Embankment in Saint Petersburg, facing the Winter Palace. Saint-Petersburg, Universitetskaya Naberazhnaya, 3, 199034, Russia. http://www.kunstkamera.ru/en/

American Museum of the House Cat

Location: Sylva, North Carolina

The World's Weirdest Museums

American Museum of the House Cat was founded by cat lover Harold Sims. The former biology professor has collected a huge array of cat-theme exhibits, such as a mummified cat dating back to ancient Egypt, handmade carousel cats, cat paintings, glass and ceramic statues, cat theme jewelry, vintage pet store advertisements, cartoon cats, and antique toys. Additionally, there are lots of photos of cats and cats with their owners, including one of Stalin with his cat.

The museum includes a history of the housecat through the ages and around the world, including how cats came to America.

Museum Founder and Curator, Dr. Harold Sims, has dedicated his retirement years as an advocate for the Stray, Abandoned, Feral Cats of Jackson County, North Carolina. He began rescuing cats in the mid 1990's and in 2002 opened the Catman2 Shelter, Western North Carolina's largest No Kill, Cage Free, open concept Cat's Only Shelter.

The 'Catman', as the locals know him, is a humanitarian of animal rights. The shelter has taken in and adopted more than 4,000 cats over the years. In 2017, working with Catman2 Inc., the Jackson County Animal Shelter successfully achieved the rank of a no kill shelter for cats because no healthy, adoptable cats were put to sleep in the county shelter. Proceeds from the museum go to fund the shelter.

The World's Weirdest Museums

VISITOR TIPS: The museum is open daily, except Mondays and holidays, April 1 – December 31. Guided tours are conducted in the off season by appointment. Leashed cats are permitted to join you as you tour this quirky little museum. *4704 U S Highway 441, Sylva, NC 28779.*
https://www.facebook.com/americanmuseumofthehousecat

International Spy Museum

Location: Washington, DC

The World's Weirdest Museums

The International Spy Museum may not be weird, per se, but it is definitely unique and intriguing. The International Spy Museum is "dedicated to the tradecraft, history and contemporary role of espionage," featuring the largest collection of international espionage artifacts currently on public display.

The museum opened on July 19, 2002 and moved to L'Enfant Plaza on May 12, 2019. It extends across two large floors of this contemporary building. Discover how the work of real spies has changed history and continues to play a critical role in national security.

Listen to real stories from real spies. The Spy Museum works closely with former international intelligence leaders to educate visitors while making it a thrilling experience. Learn about the life of spies and the history of espionage worldwide.

Test your own spy skills through RFID experiences, explore interactive exhibits and see real tools of this clandestine trade. Undercover Mission is a really cool spy game that most visitors love to play.

The World's Weirdest Museums

VISITOR TIPS: The plaza is south of the Smithsonian Castle on the National Mall and directly across from the United States Postal Service Headquarters in Southwest Washington, DC. Discounted rates for students, seniors, law enforcement, and military. Children under six are free. www.spymuseum.com. The museum is popular so expect large crowds, especially during peak vacation times. There is a gift shop with fun spy souvenirs. Check out this multimedia presentation at
https://www.spymuseum.org/multimedia/

FYI: The Spy Museum is not to be confused with the CIA Museum. The CIA Museum is a national archive for the collection, preservation, documentation and exhibition of intelligence artifacts, culture, and history. The 3,500+ item collection is held in trust for the American people, but the museum is not open to the public. However, the CIA Museum offers some public exhibitions in partnership with the Presidential Libraries and other major museums and institutions. The National Cryptologic Museum in Maryland is NSA's equivalent to the CIA Museum and is open to the public. These two museums serve as the main government museums for the collection and preservation in the U.S. Intelligence Community.
https://www.cia.gov/about-cia/cia-museum

Canadian Potato Museum

Location: Prince Edward Island, Canada

In case you're worried you might not be able to find the **Canadian Potato Museum**, you can't miss the fourteen-foot fiberglass potato on display in front of the museum. It may surprise you to learn that potatoes are abundant on Prince Edward Island.

The museum features potato-related exhibits and a café that features novel potato products, such as potato cinnamon buns, loaded spuds, potato soup, and potato fudge. There is an antique farm machine gallery,

The World's Weirdest Museums

blacksmith workshop, carriage-making workshop, and gift shop.

The "Amazing Potato Exhibit" and the "Potato Interpretive Center" take you on "a journey through time, learning about the potato from its beginning as a wild food source in South America, to the fourth largest commercial crop in the world.

There are several historical buildings on the grounds, including the Heritage Chapel, Log Barn, Little Red Schoolhouse, and the Telephone Switchboard office.

VISITOR TIPS: Open mid-May to mid-October. The Potato Blossom Festival is held every July. This event includes fireworks, a banquet, and a Miss Potato contest. PEI Potato Country Kitchen is open mid-June – mid-September. Reduced rates for seniors and families. 1 Dewar Lane, O'Leary PE C0B 1V0. https://www.canadianpotatomuseum.info/

FYI: There is also a potato museum in the U.S. The Idaho Potato Museum is in Blackfoot, Idaho. It shares all things potato, including how to farm them, the different types of potatoes, and potato foods. One of the highlights of this museum is the world's largest Pringle®. 130 Northwest Main Street
Blackfoot, Idaho 83221.
https://idahopotatomuseum.com/

The World's Weirdest Museums

More Food Museums…

Colman's Mustard Shop and Museum (Norwich, UK)

Frietmuseum (Bruges, Belgium) This museum is devoted to French fries, which Belgium claims to have created—not France.

Udon Museum (Kyoto, Japan)
There are 35 types of udon noodles, all of which can be seen in the museum. Each region in Japan has its own udon and its own way of eating them.

Dutch Cheese Museum (Alkmaar, Netherlands)

York's Chocolate Story (York, England)
This chocolate-themed museum highlights how the chocolate industry transformed this northern English city.

Kimchi Museum (Seoul, South Korea)
It's the only food museum in this country.

Currywurst Museum (Berlin, Germany)
European Bread Museum (Ebergötzen, Germany)

Southern Food and Beverage Museum (New Orleans, Louisiana)
This museum is all about southern cuisine and includes the American Cocktail gallery.

Museum of Olive Oil Production (Lesvos, Greece)

The World's Weirdest Museums

Mutter Museum

Location: Philadelphia, Pennsylvania

The **Mütter Museum** boasts an unusual collection of specimens and objects pertaining to the history of medicine and anatomy. Their collection ranges from 7th century BCE to the present, but most of the collection dates from the mid-19th century to the early 20th century.

There are some non-human specimens, but mostly the museum features human specimens, including more than 100 skulls. There are anatomical models, wet specimens, and medieval-looking medical tools, including a Civil War-era amputation kit.

The purpose of the museum is to educate visitors on the human body.

The World's Weirdest Museums

VISITOR TIPS: Open daily seven days a week, except on holidays. Discounts given to military, seniors, youth, and students. Children five and under are free. Also, discounts are extended on Mondays and Tuesdays. 19 S 22nd Street, Philadelphia, Pennsylvania 19103.
www.muttermuseum.org

National Museum of Funeral History

Location: Houston, Texas

The World's Weirdest Museums

The **National Museum of Funeral History** has a slogan, *"Any day above ground is a good one."* Hard to argue with that logic!

Dating back to 1922, this museum boasts the country's largest collection of funeral artifacts, including memorabilia from Michael Jackson's memorial service and from many presidential funerals. It is a surprisingly interesting place, especially the hearses and fantasy coffins exhibits. There are fifteen permanent exhibits ranging from ancient Egypt to modern day funeral practices, as well as special exhibits. Click on this link to see a photo gallery of the museum, https://www.nmfh.org/exhibits/image-gallery. I recommend the Day of the Dead exhibit, Tomb of the Unknown Soldier exhibit, and the antique hearses. The National Museum of Funeral History is designed as a self-guided experience, however many groups prefer to schedule a guided tour.

 The gift shop offers many novelty gifts, as you can imagine. One such item is a t-shirt that reads *"In dog years, I'm dead!"*

 The Museum boasts 30,500-square-foot exhibit space (and can be rented for private events) and 10,000 square feet in dining, kitchen, meeting space, 100-seat auditorium, private boardroom and classrooms. The most commonly hosted events include non-traditional weddings, workshops, over the hill birthday parties, receptions, Halloween parties, and memorial services.

The World's Weirdest Museums

VISITOR TIPS: Discounted admission is offered to SCI employees, seniors, military, and youth. Children five and under are free. The museum is open seven days a week and is handicapped accessible. 415 Barren Springs Drive. Houston, Texas 77090-5918.
https://www.nmfh.org/

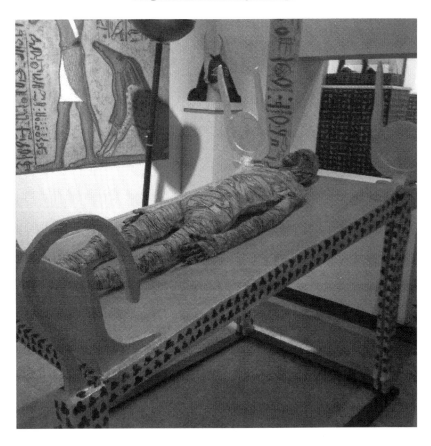

FYI: Collection of Funeral Carriages and Hearses (Barcelona, Spain) is dedicated to transportation used throughout the history of funerals.
https://irbarcelona.org/barcelona-museums/funeral-carriages-hearses-collection/

New Orleans Historic Voodoo Museum

Location: New Orleans, Louisiana

The Voodoo Museum was established in 1972. It showcases the origins of voodoo, as well as the items used to perform these rituals and cast spells. Its purpose is to educate and entertain visitors about the culture of voodoo and its link to New Orleans. The museum is small but packed with intriguing items, including voodoo dolls, relics, artifacts, and paintings.

VISITOR TIPS: The tour is self-guided. Psychic readings are offered and there is a gift shop that sells voodoo items. Discounted admission for seniors, military, students, and children 12 and under. 724

The World's Weirdest Museums

Dumaine Street, New Orleans, Louisiana 70116 (between Bourbon Street and Royal Street, in the heart of the French Quarter).
https://www.voodoomuseum.com/

FYI: The Voodoo Museum offers Walking Tours to the nearby St. Louis Cemetery (the City of the Dead) and the famous tomb of Marie Laveau.

Museum of Death

Location: Hollywood, California

The World's Weirdest Museums

The Museum of Death was established in 1995 when JD Healy and Cathee Shultz decided to make death their life's work. It houses the world's largest collection of serial killer artwork, execution devices, letters written by murderers, mortician and coroners' instruments, Manson Family memorabilia, Helter Skelter memorabilia, Black Dahlia, Heaven's Gate Cult suicide, pet death taxidermy, crime scene photographs and many more death theme items.

One of the strangest and most gruesome things in

the museum is an embalming video. Another disturbing item is the preserved (guillotined) head of Henri Desire Landru, a.k.a. the Bluebeard of France. He brutally murdered more than 200 women before being executed in 1922. There is a gallery of paintings and drawings done by murderers who were incarcerated on Death Row, including the Son of Sam.

The museum's building once served as a sound studio is where Pink Floyd recorded their legendary album, "The Wall"). Some rooms actually have sand in the walls, so it is an eerily quiet place.

The World's Weirdest Museums

VISITOR TIPS: It is a self-guided tour that generally takes one hour. There is no age minimum but the museum advises against bringing young children. Everyone under the age of 18 must be accompanied by a parent.

There are currently two museum locations- 6031 Hollywood Blvd in Hollywood, CA and 227 Dauphine Street in New Orleans, LA. There is no duplication in these museums as they have completely different exhibits. Both are open seven days a week. Large bags and backpacks will be held for safekeeping. The museum has a strict policy against photography, cell phone usage, eating, smoking, drinking, and weapon possession while inside the premises.

www.museumofdeath.net

Museum of Clean

Location: Pocatello, Idaho

The World's Weirdest Museums

The Museum of Clean houses cleaning-related products, including vintage vacuums and artwork. Yes, there are cleaning-themed paintings and sculptures! The size of this museum is astonishing. It is a 75,000-square foot complex spread out across six levels.

As you can imagine, the founder of this museum is a clean 'freak'. Don Aslett says his mother married his father because she was impressed with how clean he was. He kept himself and his belongings properly neat and tidy. His mother kept a clean house, a perfect-looking yard, and their clothes were always so clean and crisp they looked new.

So it is no surprise that by the time Aslett was a young man, he began a cleaning company. He did so well that he began giving talks and writing books about cleaning. He began collecting cleaning products and the idea of opening a museum came to him as his collection grew to a substantial size. By 2006, Aslett possessed 250 vintage vacuum cleaners, as well as many other cleaning tools.

By 2011, the museum had to upsize to a bigger facility that was renovated to be eco-friendly. By 2018, the museum had acquired 1,000 vacuums dating from 1869 to 1969, including the world's first vacuum. This 1912 vacuum required two people to operate it. One person had to stand on it and operate the tow alternating the bellows with his feet, while the other person pulled the head of the vacuum hose along the carpet.

Also, there is a 1900 Old Store exhibit featuring cleaning products in vintage containers with price stickers showing what they cost when they originally

The World's Weirdest Museums

sold. Some are so outdated that a plaque has to explain what they were once used for. Some of the most archaic-looking items include vintage washing machines and washboards. Wives will love the garage exhibit devoted to a man's clutter. Additionally, there are brooms collected from around the world (even a witch's broom), European toilets, old timey bathtubs, and more. Learn how soldiers used their helmets to clean up and even cook!

There is a restoration room and library showcasing a large collection of cleaning books and DVDs. Plus, this quirky museum has lots of hands-on, interactive exhibits for kids, including a giant ark, windmill, and Kids' Planet. There is a gift shop where you can buy a clean souvenir.

VISITOR TIPS: Open Tuesday – Saturday. Discounts for families and children. 711 S. 2nd Avenue, Pocatello, Idaho 83201.
http://museumofclean.com.s158603.gridserver.com/

Vienna Undertakers' Museum

Location: Vienna, Austria

The World's Weirdest Museums

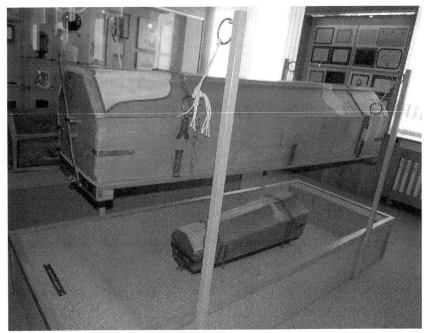

The Reusable Coffin

The **Vienna Undertakers' Museum** features roughly 1,000 items related to Viennese funeral traditions, such as hearses, exquisite coffins, expensive cremation urns, and mourning attire. Tours include a chance to lie down in coffin, if you are comfortable with that.

Back in the day, funerals were a BIG DEAL, especially in parts of Europe. Attendance was high and a lot of money was spent on them. When the Austro-

Hungarian Empire was at its peak people paid heavily to make sure they received a grand send-off.

In the 1900s, more than eighty private funeral companies competed for the business of burying Viennese citizens in one of the 52 area cemeteries. In 1951, the Undertaking Service of Vienna (Bestattung Wien) became the sole provider of funeral services in the city for a long time. Even today, Bestattung is one of the biggest funeral homes in the country. They conduct thousands of services a year and produce 25,000 coffins annually. It also houses this unique museum.

The Funeral Museum was founded by them in 1967. It received a major makeover in 1987. Some of its most intriguing exhibits include a re-usable coffin proposed in 1784 by Emperor Josef II. The corpse drops through a trap door, freeing the coffin up for another recipient. The idea was to save wood, which was a precious commodity at that time. It also served to accelerate decomposition. Not surprisingly, the idea was not well received and the law was repealed within six months.

The museum features interactive exhibits and histories, including the "Viennese Cult of the Dead," and Viennese mourning ceremonies. At one time, being buried alive was a real concern. Being unconscious or in a coma was sometimes mistaken as being dead. The affluent used certain safeguards to ensure this didn't happen to their loved ones. A cord was attached to the hand of the deceased that was connected to a bell located above ground. Grave watchers were hired or family members sometimes sat by the graves for a couple of days. If the bell began ringing, you better begin digging!

Also, some Viennese stipulated in their will that after death they should be stabbed in the heart with a sword. Even today the city's hospital is occasionally instructed to administer a lethal injection after death to avoid premature burial.

VISITOR TIPS: Ages 18 and under are free. Closed on weekends and holidays. Simmeringer Hauptstrasse 234, A-1110 Wien. Vienna, Austria.
www.bestattungsmuseum.at

Sitting Coffin

The World's Weirdest Museums

Sulabh International Museum of Toilets

Location: New Delhi, India

The Sulabh International Museum of Toilets was established to chronicle the history and importance of toilets in our society. But before you scoff at this museum, you should check out their displays showing how things were before the invention of the septic system.

Known in the U.S. as bathrooms, they are called water closets (W.C.) in other parts of the world. Whatever you call them, you can't overstate their importance!

The World's Weirdest Museums

Exhibits include fancy hand-carved and painted urinals and commodes. Emperors once had toilet pots made of pure gold and silver. There is a picture of a medieval mobile commode in the shape of a treasure chest, which was used while hunting and camping.

The Museum has a stock of interesting anecdotes associated with the development of toilets. The national flags of different countries, from where the pictures of toilets have been collected, are also displayed. In case you're wondering who would be interested, the museum attracts thousands of visitors a year from all over the world. It has been featured in many media stories and now a book has been written that features a chapter about it!

The museum is the brainchild of Dr. Bindeshwar Pathak, Sociologist, Social Reformer, and Founder of the Sulabh Sanitation Movement. He sent letters requesting information for the museum. More than 60 Embassies and High Commissions responded to the request and sent documents, photographs, drawings, and objects.

Visitor Tips: Open daily, except holidays, free of charge and free parking. Sulabh Bhawan, RZ-83, Palam Dabri Marg, Kali Nagar, Mahavir Enclave I, Mahavir Enclave Part 1, Mahavir Enclave, New Delhi, India 110045. http://www.sulabhtoiletmuseum.org/

Click here to take a virtual tour of the museum, http://www.sulabhtoiletmuseum.org/visit/virtual-tour-of-museum/

WEIRD FACT: Approximately 40,000 Americans are injured by toilets each year.

The World's Weirdest Museums

The Museum of Icelandic Sorcery & Witchcraft

Location: Holmavik, Iceland

The **Museum of Icelandic Sorcery & Witchcraft** is located in a small town on the western coast of Iceland. Many tourists go out of their way to visit this unique museum, which is a popular tourist attraction.

A caped skeleton, who looks like he has arisen from the stone floor, welcomes visitors and sets the tone for the museum.

At one time, witchcraft was widespread in Europe, especially in Iceland. In the 16th and 17th

The World's Weirdest Museums

centuries, witch-hunting was common. Persons believed to be witches or sorcerers were burned alive. While witches and sorcerers were predominantly women in most of Europe, the majority were men in Iceland.

They were accused of putting curses on their neighbors, causing them to become ill or to die. Some were accused of trying to seduce women, harm livestock, and even change the weather. This was done using magical runes and placing them strategically.

But this museum is more than witchcraft and sorcery. It shares the dark history of Europe, especially Iceland.

VISITOR TIPS: The museum is open every day and there is a restaurant on site. Reservations are required for dinner. Discounts are extended to seniors and the disabled. Admission is free to 17 and under. Hofoagata 8-10, Holmavik 510, Iceland. http://www.galdrasyning.is/

Museum of Sex

Location: New York City, New York

The World's Weirdest Museums

The Museum of Sex opened in 2002. It is a cultural and educational experience that mixes science, history, and art exhibits. The exhibits are meant to be fun and highlight variety of fun and different perspectives on sexuality, not just in America but worldwide.

Since its inception, the Museum of Sex has created nearly three dozen exhibits and a half dozen virtual installations to stimulate dialog and educate the public. Interesting lectures and special events are held, as well.

The Museum's permanent collection includes

20,000 works of art, photography, costumes, inventions, and more. There is an impressive research and multimedia library.

This is not some silly or frivolous museum. It has garnered accolades from numerous academic institutions and major media, including *Time*, CNN, and *The New York Times*.

There is a museum gift shop full of souvenirs for those who dare!

VISITOR TIPS: Open seven days a week. Discounts available to seniors, military, and students. You must be eighteen years old to enter the museum. 233 Fifth Avenue, New York, NY 10016.
https://www.museumofsex.com/

```
WEIRD FACT: If a female ferret does
  not have sex for a year, she will
                die.
```

The World's Weirdest Museums

Mummy Museum

Location: Guanajuato, Mexico

The Mummy Museum is quite an unusual museum. It displays the mummy remains of Guanajuato residents who died during a cholera outbreak in 1833. At that time, a local tax had to be paid for burial. If the tax was not paid, the remains were disinterred and stored in an ossuary building near the Santa Paula Cemetery.

The mummies were exhumed between 1870 – 1958. When they began removing some corpses, they discovered they were well preserved. The altitude and climate of this region created a natural mummification process. But upon closer examination, it was discovered that the bodies had been embalmed to some extent.

As word spread about the mummies, curious tourists asked to see them. By the 1900s, employees charged three pesos to show them to tourists. This eventually led to the creation of a museum to house the one hundred mummies, including the smallest mummy in the world. Some of the mummies are still wearing remnants of clothing. It is creepy but also intriguing.

The mummies you'll see on display have not been retouched, dressed, or "fixed" in any way: you'll see them as they were buried, Babies and infants were probably buried with their eyes left open and their hands folded in prayer; it was expected that "Little Angels" would fly straight to heaven where the Virgin awaited them.

VISITOR TIPS: Open seven days a week. Not recommended for children. Admission is discounted late in the day. Municipal Pantheon Esplanade, Downtown C.P. 36000, Guanajuato, Mexico.
http://www.momiasdeguanajuato.gob.mx/

FYI: Guanajuato City is the capital of Guanajuato and is a UNESCO World Heritage Site. It is a former silver mining town and a battle site during the Mexican War of Independence.

The World's Weirdest Museums

Torture Museum

Location: Amsterdam, Netherlands

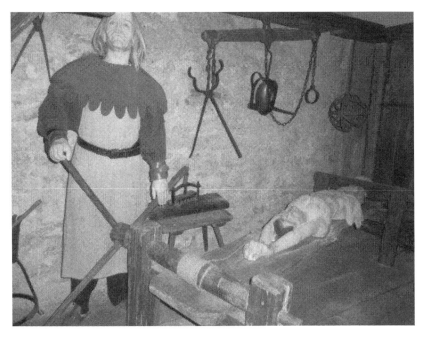

The **Torture Museum** displays more than 100 torture devices throughout many gruesomely, fascinating exhibits. These exhibits include life-size wax figures, torture tools, period props, and sound effects. Vlad the Impaler "Dracula" and Iron Maiden are just a couple of their popular exhibits.

Common torture devices in the Middle Ages in Europe included the guillotine, inquisition chair, skullcracker, the rack, thumb screws, and the garrote.

The World's Weirdest Museums

The point of this museum is to share Europe's history, at least as it pertains to crime and punishment, and do so in a way that is both informative and entertaining.

VISITOR TIPS: The Torture Museum provides guided tours for groups. Open seven days a week. Discounts are given to children. Damrak 33, 1012 LK, 1012 LK Amsterdam (opposite the flower market).
http://www.torturemuseum.com/

British Lawnmower Museum

Location: Southport, Great Britain

The World's Weirdest Museums

The British Lawnmower Museum is home to vintage lawnmowers, antique garden equipment, related documents, and more. It was the brainchild of ex-racing champion, Brian Radam. His family's business, Lawnmowerworld, led him to open this unique museum.

The 600+ items displayed are from the Industrial revolution in 1799 to the present day. I think the best exhibits are 'Lawnmowers of the Rich and Famous' and 'Lawnmower Racing'. Lawnmowers of the Rich and Famous Exhibit includes Prince Charles and Princess

Diana, Brian May, Nicholas Parsons, Eric Morcambe, Hilda Ogden, Alan Titchmarsh and more.

The modern sport of lawn mower racing originated one night in a pub in 1973. While knocking back a few pints in Cricketers Arms in West Sussex, Jim Gavin and his friends came up with the idea to race lawn mowers.

The first British Grand Prix meeting for lawn mowers ran at Wisborough Green that same year with thirty-five drivers entering the race. They drove mowers ranging from a 1923 Atco to a brand new 8-horsepower Wheel horse tractor. There were races for run behind mowers, towed seat mowers and the type you sit on top of. Over the years the sport has grown in popularity and is outside of Britain. I saw a lawnmower race in South Carolina and it was a hoot!

The World's Weirdest Museums

Be sure to check out **the first Solar Powered ROBOT mower,** Ransome Spider Robot features FOUR-WHEEL DRIVE, FOUR-WHEEL STEERING, AND 24HP twin cylinder Kawasaki engine. It can be operated remotely from up to one kilometer or less than one mile away. *The cost?* Approximately £26,000!

VISITOR TIPS: 106-112 Shakespeare Street, Southport, Merseyside PR8 5AJ Great Britain.
http://www.lawnmowerworld.co.uk/

British Lawn Mower Racing Association.
http://www.blmra.co.uk/

United States Lawnmower Racing Association, www.letsmow.com

FYI: The lawnmower was patented by Edwin Beard Budding in 1830. At the time people thought he was crazy to invent such a thing, so he had to test the machine at night so no one could see him.

The World's Weirdest Museums

Vent Haven Ventriloquist museum

Location: Fort Mitchell, Kentucky

Vent Haven Museum is the world's only museum dedicated to ventriloquism. Its purpose is to educate the public about ventriloquism, including its origins and how dummies are made. This unique museum contains more than 900 dummies from the 19th, 20th, and 21st centuries.

Vent Haven Museum was founded by Ohio native William Shakespeare "W.S." Berger. Oddly, he was not a professional ventriloquist. But he did have

The World's Weirdest Museums

an interest in dummies. He bought his first dummy, Tommy Baloney, in 1910. By the early 1940s, his collection was impressive—and had outgrown his home storage capacity. He renovated his garage, and in 1962, he built a second building.

From the late 1940's until 1960, W.S. was the president of the International Brotherhood of Ventriloquists. His leadership helped the organization grow from around 300 members to more than 1,000. He published a monthly magazine, *The Oracle*, for the organization's membership. Berger corresponded with ventriloquists worldwide, writing dozens of letters every week.

Before his death, Berger set up a charitable foundation to make sure that his museum continued to operate as a non-profit organization.

VISITOR TIPS: Vent Haven Museum is open by appointment only May 1 through September 30. Also, there are Open House dates throughout the year. There is no fee but donations are greatly appreciated. 33 West Maple Avenue, Fort Mitchell, Kentucky 41011 (five miles south of Cincinnati, Ohio)
https://www.venthaven.org/

FYI: There is an annual Vent Haven Ventriloquist Convention.

The World's Weirdest Museums

Avanos Hair Museum

Location: Avanos, Turkey

The Avanos hair museum may be the strangest museum included in this book and that's saying a lot! The museum, located in a small cave underneath a pottery shop owned by Chez Galip, is full of hair samples. Each sample also has the name and address of the person who donated the hair. This adds up to more than 16,000 women from across the globe.

The museum was founded many years ago when one of Galip's friends had to leave Avanos. This was very hard on him. He became very sad. Before her

The World's Weirdest Museums

departure, he asked his friend for a keepsake and she gave Galip a clipping of her hair. He proudly displayed it in his shop. Naturally, people asked about the hair and its history was explained to them. This strange story became well known through the years. Tourists who visited this part of Cappadocia began leaving a 'keepsake', as well.

Women leave hair for more than sentimental reasons. Hair samples are selected twice a year by one of Galip's customers in June and December. Those chosen are invited to return for a free Cappadocia vacation and may attend workshops with the master potter.

If you get a chance to visit the museum, you will see that every surface, except for the floor, is covered with the hair samples. While some women only leave their address, others write little notes and even attach photos.

The museum is listed in the Guinness Book of World Records.

VISITOR TIPS: Yeni Mh. Hasan Kalesi Mevkii No. 3 Avanos/Nevsehir, Turkey.

https://www.chezgalip.com/the-hair-museum-of-avanos/

The World's Weirdest Museums

Cupnoodles Museum

Location: Osaka, Japan

Cupnoodles Museum (also known as Momofuku Ando Instant Ramen Museum) was established by Momofuku Ando, who created instant noodles and the brands, Top Ramen and Cup Noodles. Ando lived until the ripe, old age of 96. He claimed that the secret of his long life was playing golf and eating Chicken ramen almost every day. He was said to have eaten instant ramen until the day he died. This is a favorite meal for college students worldwide who are on a budget.

The museum is much more than bags of

The World's Weirdest Museums

noodles. It includes a ramen workshop where visitors can make their own instant noodles. The Magical Table is an innovative way to learn all about these noodles through fun quizzes. The Exhibition of Instant Noodles is a colorful exhibit that shows which countries eat the most noodles and which flavors are most consumed. The Instant Noodles Tunnel showcases hundreds of noodle packages.

Additionally, there is a Tasting Room where visitors can buy noodles out of vending machines and enjoy them in a dining area. Of course, there is a gift shop where souvenirs of your visit can be acquired.

VISITOR TIPS: Free Admission. 8-25 Masumi-cho, Ikeda-shi, Osaka 563-0041 Japan https://www.cupnoodles-museum.jp/en/osaka_ikeda/

WEIRD FACT: Human birth control pills work on gorillas.

The World's Weirdest Museums

Meguro Parasitological Museum

Location: Tokyo, Japan

The Meguro Parasitological Museum exhibits 300 parasite specimens and related items. This strange museum was established in 1953 by Dr. Satoru Kamegai. Believe it or not, this parasite museum has grown increasingly popular as an offbeat attraction.

    The privately owned research museum includes two levels of exhibits, such as "Diversity of Parasites" and "Human and Zoonotic Parasites", as well as educational films and maps. The museum only displays a fraction of its collection, which includes 60,000

The World's Weirdest Museums

parasite specimens, 50,000 papers, and 6,000 books on parasitology and parasitic diseases.

The museum's prize attraction is a tapeworm. It is the world's longest tapeworm at nearly 9 meters or 29 feet.

VISITOR TIPS: Free admission. Closed Mondays, Tuesdays, and holidays. There is a museum shop that sells quirky souvenirs. 4-1-1 Shimomeguro, Meguro-ku, Tokyo 153-0064, JAPAN.

https://www.kiseichu.org/e-top

FYI: A tapeworm is a parasite that lives in hosts like pets, farm animals, and humans.

Kansas Barbed Wire Museum

Location: La Crosse, Kansas

The World's Weirdest Museums

The **Kansas Barbed Wire Museum** is devoted to educating the public on the history of barbed wire. Yes, you read correctly—barbed wire. The facility displays 2,400 types of barbed wire and discusses its importance in taming the Wild West. In addition to barbed wire, related tools and equipment are exhibited.

Joseph Glidden invented barbed wire fencing in 1874. He patented his invention and soon it was a multi-million dollar business. Their slogan was *"Cheaper than dirt and stronger than steel."*

The Kansas Barbed Wire Collectors Association

was founded on May 17, 1964. It was soon discovered that there were many amateur collectors of this fencing wire. With all this interest in barbed wire, three visionary LaCrosse businessmen (Ivan Krug, Roy Ehly, and Bill Robbins) met to discuss organizing all these collectors.

On Sunday, January 8, 1967 a group of barbed wire collectors met at the LaCrosse Country Club. During the meeting, collectors were given the opportunity to display their collections, discuss the hobby, and swap pieces of barbed wire. That afternoon the Kansas Barbed Wire Collectors Association (KBWCA) was born, the second association of its kind in the United States.

The first KBWCA Swap and Sell show was held on May 6-7, 1967 at the Rush County Fairgrounds in LaCrosse. Show hosts had initially planned for 44 display tables, but by 10:00 a.m. Saturday, they were sold out and had to secure additional tables and display space. Before the show was over, the Exhibit Building was overflowing with displays. Collectors were in attendance from Texas, Oklahoma, Missouri, Nebraska, Colorado, South Dakota, and several towns in Kansas. Between 1500 and 2000 people attended.

In its first year, the KBWCA had 133 members. In a few years, it grew to nearly 350 members from 18 different states. Magazines across the country ran stories about the hobby. In 1969, Ivan Krug, made an appearance on *The Tonight Show Starring Johnny Carson* to talk about the hobby and to give Johnny an opportunity to try his hand at splicing barbed wire.

Over the next few years, interest in the hobby continued to grow. Other collectors associations sprang up across the country. Collectors began to amass huge and valuable collections of barbed wire and related tools. Some realized a need for a permanent home to exhibit a sampling of these unique collections.

The same group of LaCrosse businessmen, along with a few others, began planning the first barbed wire museum. The LaCrosse Chamber of Commerce purchased an old storefront on Main Street and offered the front room to the collectors. News of the unique museum spread like wildfire. In May of 1970, Charles Kuralt brought his *On the Road* crew and filmed a segment in LaCrosse.

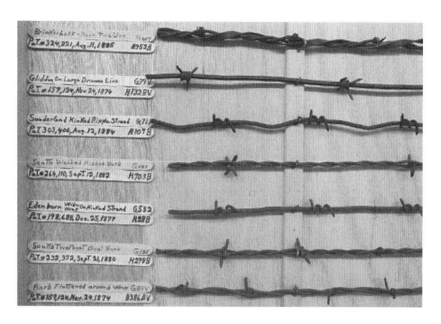

By 1971, the *Barbed Wire Museum* was officially dedicated. With barbed wire collecting now synonymous with LaCrosse, the small western Kansas community became known as *The Barbed Wire Capital of the World*.

The World's Weirdest Museums

By 1990, the museum had outgrown its location. A new museum was built later that year. At the same time while the Kansas museum was under construction, another barbed wire museum, *The Devils Rope Museum*, was being opened in a former factory in the small town of McLean, Texas. A Texas newspaper reporter did a story about the two museums opening simultaneously and decided that the two groups must be feuding. Other papers picked up the story. Representatives from each of the institutions met and decided to give them what they want and a "friendly feud" ensued.

To settle the feud, organizers planned a gunfight during the 1990 wire show in the *Dodge House* hotel in Dodge City, Kansas with the victor claiming the title of *Barbed Wire Capital of the World*. When the smoke cleared, LaCrosse had retained its title. News spread and once again the hobby was featured in large newspapers, national magazines such as *The Smithsonian*, and on the *CBS Evening News*.

Over the next decade, it was realized that an

international association was needed. An organizational meeting was held in Dodge City, Kansas and the *Antique Barbed Wire Society* (ABWS) was born. A home base was needed for the new society and LaCrosse was naturally chosen.

In May of 2005, the new facility was completed featuring a research library housing the largest collection of fencing-related materials in existence, a community room, and storage facility. The *Kansas Barbed Wire Museum* and the ABWS continue to receive new artifacts for their collections. If you go, don't miss the Diorama and the Evolution of Barbed Wire exhibit.

Thanks to the Internet, the hobby is discovering a previously unknown network of collectors throughout the world. Wire collectors across the United States still get together the first weekend in May to swap and sell barbed wire.

The World's Weirdest Museums

VISITOR TIPS: Open daily May 1 – Labor Day. No admission fee.
120 W. 1st Street, La Crosse, Kansas 67548.
http://www.rushcounty.org/BarbedWireMuseum/index.html.
Check out a virtual tour at
http://www.rushcounty.org/BarbedWireMuseum/BWvirtual.html

Museum of Broken Relationships

Location: Zagreb, Croatia & Los Angeles, California

The World's Weirdest Museums

The Museum of Broken Relationships began as a traveling exhibit highlighting failed relationships, but grew into a permanent museum.

The museum collects things that are sent anonymously with stories about what the items are and what they meant to the failed relationship.

There is also a confessional book in the back of the building where you can write about your own failed relationships and a wall where you can fill in the blanks with the provided pieces of paper and then stick them on the wall.

It's a bit heartbreaking but maybe also comforting to know you are not alone, that many others have experienced the same thing. But everyone has a unique item signifying the broken relationship. These range from articles of clothing to more graphic symbols. Some exhibits are a bit scary or downright weird.

VISITOR TIPS: The museum is located on Hollywood Blvd, and there is not much street parking available. I would recommend heading to Hollywood and Highland where there is a big parking lot under the mall. This is a great place to park and to explore all that Hollywood Blvd has to offer. You can walk to the museum from here. It is one block east of Highland. Open seven days a week. Discounts given to students, military, disabled, and seniors. 6751 Hollywood Blvd., Los Angeles, California 90028. https://brokenships.com/ and http://brokenships.la/

The World's Weirdest Museums

FYI: There is also a Museum of Broken Relationships in Europe, established 2010. It is open year round except holidays. Ćirilometodska 2, 10000, Zagreb, Croatia.

Bunny Museum

Location: Pasadena, California

The World's Weirdest Museums

The **Bunny Museum** was established in 1998. Their collection includes ceramic bunnies, toys, antiques, stuffed bunnies, collectibles, jewelry, Rose Parade float bunnies, cookie jar bunnies, and much, much, more, including a giant rabbit topiary on the front lawn.

It holds the Guinness World Record for 'owning the most bunny items in the world' with 35,000 items spread out across two floors. Be sure to check out their Gooba and Chamber of Hop Horrors exhibits.

Their slogan is *"The Hoppiest Place in the World."*

VISITOR TIPS: Open seven days a week. Discounts given to seniors, children, and military. Children four and under are free. 2605 N. Lake Avenue, Altadena, CA 91001 https://www.thebunnymuseum.com

The World's Weirdest Museums

International UFO Museum

Location: Roswell, New Mexico

The **International UFO Museum and Research Center** chronicles the history of sightings of unidentified flying objects (UFOs). While it largely focuses on the famous 1947 Roswell Crash, it also has a lot of information and exhibits on other incidents in the U.S. and across the globe. Founded in 1991, the nonprofit museum also boasts a research library and cool gift shop. It is housed in a former 1930s movie theater.

The World's Weirdest Museums

*VISITOR TIPS: Open seven days a week. Discounts given to military, first responders, seniors, and children. 114 N Main St.
Roswell, New Mexico 88203.
https://www.roswellufomuseum.com/*

FYI: There is an annual UFO convention. The National UFO Conference (NUFOC) is an annual conference with a mission "to present top researchers in the field of ufology who will share their ongoing and current research." The National UFO Conference is the longest active conference in the United States presenting information on the UFO phenomenon.

Condom Museum

Location: Nothaburi, Thailand

The **Condom Museum** shows the evolution of condoms through the years (for those who care). Founded by Thailand's Ministry of Health, the museum's main purpose is to overcome the negative connotation of condom use in this country, which is ironic given the fact that Thailand is one of the world's largest producers of condoms and also because Thailand is known for its illicit nightlife, especially in Bangkok.

The World's Weirdest Museums

VISITOR TIPS: Open Monday – Friday. Free. It is a small museum tucked away and a bit hard to find. The museum is in the back of the ministry in building #9. You need to get permission from the department head upon arrival in order to gain entrance to the museum." Ministry of Public Health, Building 9, Department of Medical Sciences. Talat Khwan Mueang Nonthaburi 11000. Bangkok, Thailand.

https://www.museumthailand.com/en/museum/Condom-Museum

Hash, Marihuana & Hemp Museum

Location: Amsterdam, Netherlands

The World's Weirdest Museums

The **Hash, Marijuana, and Hemp Museum** reveals the history of hemp and cannabis and how marijuana is cultivated.

The museum has received more than two million visitors since it opened in 1985. Dedicated to cannabis and its many uses, the museum offers visitors information about the historical and modern uses of cannabis for medicinal, spiritual and cultural purposes.

The museum also focuses on how hemp can be used for agricultural and industrial purposes, even including clothing accessories and cosmetic products made from hemp fiber in their gift shop.

The museum has more than 12,000 objects related to marijuana spread across two canal houses and there is a Vaporizer Booth where you can give it a try.

Interestingly, modern medical research reveals how cannabis could help millions of patients. However, in 1880 cannabis was an everyday medicine in the Western world. The use of pain relief in traditional Chinese medicine goes back even thousands of years. And have you noticed all the hemp shops and hemp products available these days?

A free audio tour is available and a unique temporary exhibition can be seen regularly.

The World's Weirdest Museums

VISITOR TIPS: Free with an Amsterdam City Card and for children 13 and younger. The museum is handicapped accessible. Oudezijds Achterburgwal 148 1012 DV Amsterdam. www.hashmuseum.com

FYI: The museum is also in Barcelona. Carrer Ample 35

Barcelona, Spain.

Dog Collar Museum

Location: Kent, England

The World's Weirdest Museums

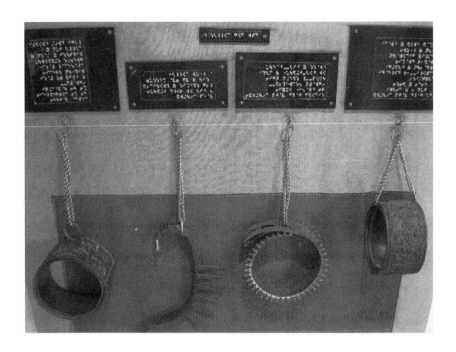

The Dog Collar Museum is a unique collection of roughly 100 rare and valuable collars that were collected by Irish scholar and historian, John Hunt, and his wife, Gertrude. It is also endowed by the Leeds Castle Foundation. The museum features canine neckwear spanning five centuries.

In the 15th, 16th, and 17th centuries, the forests of Europe were full of predators that posed a serious threat to hunting dogs. To protect their beloved dogs, hunters would fit the dogs with thick iron collars covered in impressive spikes.

By the 18th century, dog collars became more decorative than functional. These ornate collars featured velvet, baroque leather, and the royal owners' coat of arms.

The museum receives a half million visitors annually from near and far. It is the world's only dog collar museum.

The World's Weirdest Museums

VISITOR TIPS: The museum is inside the castle's former stable. Leeds Castle is in Kent, England, five miles southeast of Maidstone. It is built on islands in a lake formed by the River Len to the east of the Village of Leeds. Castle admission tickets grant **free repeat visits for a whole year** *from the date of issue Discounts are given to seniors, disabled, families, students, and children. Ages four and younger are free.* <u>Broomfield, Maidstone ME17 1PL</u> C <u>https://www.leeds-castle.com/Attractions/The+Castle+%26amp%3B+Exhibitions?id=p3</u>

FYI: The Smithsonian (Washington, DC) is the world's largest research and museum complex, with 19 museums and galleries, the National Zoological Park, and various research stations.

More Museums

The top ten most *popular* museums in the world are:

1. **The Louve** (Paris, France). One of the world's biggest and most visited museums was originally built as a fortress that was converted into a royal palace and then into a a 15-acre museum in 1793. The permanent collection features 380,000 works of art, but they are not all on display at the same time—thank goodness for tourists! While the collection includes European, Islamic, and Near Eastern arts and antiquities, the most famous image in the museum is Leonardo da Vinci's "Mona Lisa."
2. **The Palace Museum** (Beijing, China). Built in the early 15th century, the museum overlaps with the Forbidden City, which was home to Chinese emperors from the Ming dynasty to the early 20th century's Qing dynasty. The palace includes several

The World's Weirdest Museums

ancient structures, such as the Hall of Supreme Harmony and Hall of Preserving Harmony. Approximately one million artifacts are housed in the rooms, including statues, scrolls, porcelain, paintings, silk tapestries, and furniture. Among the major works is a 47-foot Yuan fresco originally designed for a Xinghua temple.

3. **The British Museum** (London, England). Sir Hans Sloane founded the British Museum in 1753. His collection included 71,000 books, antiquities, and other objects. Today, the British Museum features over eight million objects and about 80,000 are on display at any given time. The collection includes many famous works from around the world, including the Rosetta Stone and an Easter Island statue. The most controversial pieces, however, are the Parthenon sculptures. They were procured when the Ottoman Empire ruled Greece. Since gaining independence, Greece's government has

repeatedly requested the return of these sculptures.
4. **The National Gallery** (London, England). Since it opened in 1824, The National Gallery has expanded to include nearly twelve acres. It features pieces by Leonardo da Vinci, Van Gogh, and Titian.
5. **The Metropolitan Museum of Art** (New York, USA). The museum showcases more than two million pieces exhibited across two million square feet. In addition to paintings by Vincent van Gogh, Gustav Klimt, and Jackson Pollock, the space also houses the world's oldest surviving piano (from 1720), an Iranian storage jar that dates back to 3700 B.C., and a secretary cabinet that once belonged to Marie Antoinette.
6. The **Vatican Museums** (Vatican City, Italy). The Vatican Museums have expanded to 54 galleries that feature the Sistine Chapel ceiling by Michelangelo and "Stanze di Raffaello" by Raphael. The exhibits also include the Gallery of Maps,

The World's Weirdest Museums

the Gallery of Tapestries, and the Borgia Apartments, which were once home to Pope Alexander VI.

7. **Tate Modern** (London, England). Founded in 2000, the modern art museum's collection includes works by Auguste Rodin, Paul Klee, Pablo Picasso, and Cy Twombly.

8. **National Palace Museum** (Taipei, Taiwan). The collection features 700,000 artifacts, including Qing and Ming dynasty furniture, rare books, ceramics, carvings, and a piece of jade that's carved to resemble cabbage. Many consider the National Palace Museum to have the finest collection of Chinese art in the world.

9. **National Gallery of Art** (Washington, DC). This museum features everything from medieval to contemporary work by Pablo Picasso, Henri Matisse, Andy Warhol, and Roy Lichtenstein. One major highlight is "Ginevra de' Benci," the only painting by Leonardo da Vinci that's on permanent exhibition in the Americas.

10. **National Museum of Korea** (Seoul, South Korea). The museum exhibits antiquities, artwork, crafts, and more. The floors are divided into prehistory and ancient history, calligraphy and painting, and sculpture and crafts. Some noteworthy pieces include a fifth-century gold crown, a seventh-century bronze Buddha statue, an ornate 12th-century incense burner, and a 14th-century model of a 10-story pagoda built by monks.

FYI: If you want to find all kinds of weird stuff in one place, check out the Museum of the Weird—one of the last dime museums in the U.S. The <u>Museum of the Weird</u> includes authentic freak animals, real mummies, fiji mermaids, shrunken heads, and much more. The Museum also features paranormal phenomenon and cryptids, including Bigfoot. There is even a movie monster Chamber of Horrors 412 E. 6th Street, Austin, TX 78701.

The World's Weirdest Museums

Cool Museums for All Ages...

U.S. Space & Rocket Center (Huntsville, AL)
Musical Instrument Museum (Phoenix, AZ)
The World of Coca Cola (Atlanta, GA)
Museum of Science & Industry (Chicago, IL)
Museum of World Treasures (Wichita, KS)
Museum of the Rockies (Bozeman, MT)
Mob Museum (Las Vegas, NV)
Metropolitan Museum of Art (New York City, NY)
Cowboy Hall of Fame (Medora, ND)
Rock & Roll Fall of Fame (Cleveland, OH)
Charleston Museum (Charleston, SC)
Mammoth Site & Museum (Hot Springs, SD)
Jamestown Settlement (Jamestown, VA)
Museum of Pop Culture (Seattle, WA)
Buffalo Bill Center of the West (Cody, WY)

Coca Cola Museum

TERRANCE ZEPKE
Series Reading Order
& Guide

The World's Weirdest Museums

Series List

Most Haunted Series

Terrance Talks Travel Series

Weird & Wonderful Travels Series

Cheap Travel Series

Spookiest Series

Stop Talking Series

Carolinas for Kids Series

Ghosts of the Carolinas Series

Books & Guides for the Carolinas Series

& More Books by Terrance Zepke

≈

Introduction

Terrance Zepke studied Journalism at the University of Tennessee and later received a Master's degree in Mass Communications from the University of South Carolina. She studied parapsychology at the renowned Rhine Research Center.

Zepke spends much of her time happily traveling around the world but always returns home to the Carolinas where she lives part-time in both states. She has written hundreds of articles and more than fifty books. She is the host of *Terrance Talks Travel: Über Adventures*. Additionally, this award-winning and best-selling author has been featured in many publications and programs, such as NPR, CNN, *The Washington Post,* Associated Press, Travel with Rick Steves, Around the World, *Publishers Weekly,* World Travel & Dining with Pierre Wolfe, *San Francisco Chronicle*, Good Morning Show, *Detroit Free Press*, The Learning Channel, and The Travel Channel.

When she's not investigating haunted places, searching for pirate treasure, or climbing lighthouses, she is most likely packing for her next adventure to some far flung place, such as Reykjavik or Kwazulu Natal. Some of her favorite adventures include piranha fishing on the Amazon, shark cage diving in South Africa, hiking Peru's Inca Trail, camping in the Himalayas, dog-

The World's Weirdest Museums

sledding in the Arctic Circle, and a gorilla safari in the Congo.

Sign up for ***Terrance Talks Travel*** blog for free downloadable travel reports, adventure travel tips, and more at www.terrancetalkstravel.com.

You can follow her travel show, **TERRANCE TALKS TRAVEL: ÜBER ADVENTURES on** www.blogtalkradio.com/terrancetalkstravel or subscribe to it at **iTunes.**

Warning: Listening to this show could lead to a spectacular South African safari, hot-air ballooning over the Swiss Alps, Disney Adventures, and Tornado Tours!

≈

The World's Weirdest Museums

MOST HAUNTED SERIES

A Ghost Hunter's Guide to the Most Haunted Places in America (2012)
A Ghost Hunter's Guide to the Most Haunted Houses in America (2013)
A Ghost Hunter's Guide to the Most Haunted Hotels & Inns in America (2014)
A Ghost Hunter's Guide to the Most Haunted Historic Sites in America (2016) *A Ghost Hunter's Guide to the Most Haunted Places in the World* (2018)

The Ghost Hunter's MOST HAUNTED Box Set (3 in 1): Discover America's Most Haunted Destinations (2016)

MOST HAUNTED and SPOOKIEST Sampler Box Set: Featuring *A GHOST HUNTER'S GUIDE TO THE MOST HAUNTED PLACES IN AMERICA* and *SPOOKIEST CEMETERIES* (2017)

≈

SPOOKIEST SERIES

Spookiest Lighthouses (2013)
Spookiest Battlefields (2015)
Spookiest Cemeteries (2016)
Spookiest Objects (2017)
Spookiest Military Bases (2019)

Spookiest Box Set (3 in 1): Discover America's Most Haunted Destinations (2016)

TERRANCE TALKS TRAVEL SERIES

Terrance Talks Travel: A Pocket Guide to South Africa (2015)
Terrance Talks Travel: A Pocket Guide to African Safaris (2015)
Terrance Talks Travel: A Pocket Guide to Adventure Travel (2015)
Terrance Talks Travel: A Pocket Guide to Florida Keys (including Key West & The Everglades) (2016)
Terrance Talks Travel: The Quirky Tourist Guide to Key West (2017)
Terrance Talks Travel: The Quirky Tourist Guide to Cape Town (2017)
Terrance Talks Travel: The Quirky Tourist Guide to Reykjavik (2017)
Terrance Talks Travel: The Quirky Tourist Guide to Charleston, South Carolina (2017)
Terrance Talks Travel: The Quirky Tourist Guide to Ushuaia (2017)
Terrance Talks Travel: The Quirky Tourist Guide to Antarctica (2017)
Terrance Talks Travel: The Quirky Tourist Guide to Machu Picchu & Cuzco (Peru) 2017

African Safari Box Set: Featuring TERRANCE TALKS TRAVEL: *A Pocket Guide to South Africa* and *TERRANCE TALKS TRAVEL: A Pocket Guide to African Safaris* (2017)

Terrance Talks Travel: A Pocket Guide to East Africa's Uganda and Rwanda (2018)
Terrance Talks Travel: A Pocket Guide to New Zealand (2019)

Terrance Talks Travel: The Quirky Tourist Guide to Kathmandu (Nepal) & The Himalayas (2018)

The World's Weirdest Museums

Terrance Talks Travel: The Quirky Tourist Guide to Edinburgh (Scotland) (2018)

Terrance Talks Travel: The Quirky Tourist Guide to Marrakesh (Morocco) (2018)

Terrance Talks Travel: The Quirky Tourist Guide to Amsterdam (2018)

Terrance Talks Travel: The Quirky Tourist Guide to Queensland (2019)

≈

CHEAP TRAVEL SERIES

How to Cruise Cheap! (2017)

How to Fly Cheap! (2017)

How to Travel Cheap! (2017)

How to Travel FREE or Get Paid to Travel! (2017)

CHEAP TRAVEL SERIES (4 IN 1) BOX SET (2017)

≈

WEIRD & WONDERFUL TRAVELS SERIES

Weirdest Museums in the World (2019)

≈

The World's Weirdest Museums

STOP TALKING SERIES

Stop Talking & Start Writing Your Book (2015)
Stop Talking & Start Publishing Your Book (2015)
Stop Talking & Start Selling Your Book (2015)

Stop Talking & Start Writing Your Book Series (3 in 1) Box Set (2016)

≈

Message from the Author

The primary purpose of this guide is to introduce you to some titles you may not have known about. Another reason for it is to let you know all the ways you can connect with me. Authors love to hear from readers. We truly appreciate you more than you'll ever know. You're the reason we keep writing! Please feel free to send me a comment or question via the comment form provided on www.terrancezepke.com and www.terrancetalkstravel.com or follow me on your favorite social media. Don't forget that you can also listen to my writing podcast on iTunes, *A Writer's Journey*, or my travel show, **Terrance Talks Travel: Über Adventures** on Blog Talk Radio and iTunes. The best way to make sure you don't miss any episodes of these shows, new book releases, giveaways, my TRIP PICK OF THE WEEK, cheap travel tips, and dozens of free downloadable travel reports is to subscribe to **Terrance Talks Travel** on www.terrancetalkstravel.com.

Terrance

The World's Weirdest Museums

P.S. I would like to ask you to take a couple of minutes to share your feedback about any of my books you have read by posting a short review on your favorite bookseller's site so that other readers might discover the title too. This doesn't have to be more than a sentence or two. Authors appreciate readers more than you realize and we dearly love and depend upon your good reviews. Thank you!

FREE TRAVEL REPORTS!

Visit http://terrancezepke.com/shop/ to download dozens of free reports, such as:

*Worldwide Tipping Guide

*Travel Right (and Light!) with These Packing Hacks

*The Most Mysterious Places on Earth

*Perfect Places to Celebrate Christmas

*Five Best Hotel Rewards Programs

*Never Stand in Another Airport Security Line

*Twelve Best Places in the U.S. to Enjoy Autumn & Fall Colors

*Discover the #1 Travel Ailment, who is Most Likely to Get It (Surprise!), and How to Avoid it

...and much more!

See the next page for a sneak peek of another book in Terrance Zepke's 'most haunted' series:

A GHOST HUNTER'S GUIDE TO THE MOST HAUNTED HISTORIC SITES IN AMERICA

Now available from Safari Publishing

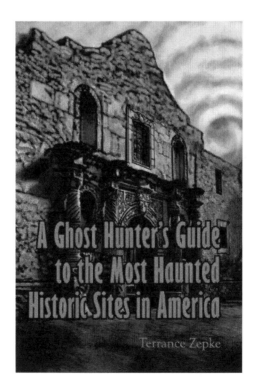

Hart Island

The World's Weirdest Museums

Hart Island

A burial trench at the potter's field on Hart Island, circa 1890 by Jacob Riis

FUN FACTS:

The island has served as home to many different enterprises and institutions through the years.

It is one of the most mysterious places in America—and haunted too!

Talk about scary; its nickname is ISLAND OF THE DEAD.

The History

What a dark and complex history this place has. It seems like it was a host to all kinds of horrible things over the years. While it may not be officially recognized as a historic site, it has great historical significance. Thousands of Confederate soldiers captured during the Civil War were imprisoned here. 3,413 men were imprisoned here with 235 of them dying while being held in this prisoner of war camp. These men were buried in Soldier's Plot on Hart Island.

The first woman buried on Hart Island was 24-year-old Louisa Van Slyke in 1869. The oldest person buried here is Ruth Proskauer Smith, who died in 2010 at the ripe old age of 102.

The World's Weirdest Museums

When the yellow fever epidemic struck New York in 1870, the island became a quarantine station. An asylum for women was established in 1885.

The United States Navy used the island as a military prison during WWII. Servicemen who were found guilty of military misconduct were sent here to serve their time. At one point, nearly 3,000 Navy, Marine, and Coast Guard personnel were incarcerated here.

The island hosted a drug rehabilitation center and a TB sanitarium. And the island was home to the Nike missile base. There was even a ball field on the island for a while. Boys and young men who were sent to the Reformatory for Misdemeanants workhouse on the island played the men stationed at the missile battery on Kratter Field. Not long after that, the reformatory was closed and so was the missile base. The reformatory closed due to misconduct. The boys were being abused and tortured by their supervisors.

For a brief time, an all-black amusement park operated on the south tip of the island. Known as the Negro Coney Island, the rides, pavilion, and boardwalk overlooked hundreds of graves and the reformatory school.

By the early 1900s, Hart Island had become one giant burial ground. Anyone in the great New York City area who could not afford a proper burial or who wasn't promptly claimed by family members were buried in mass graves on the island. Until 2007, a New York law stipulated that relatives had only forty-eight hours to claim a body. If it was not claimed by that time, the government released the body to a medical school or a mortuary school. If for whatever reason, those institutions didn't want the corpse, it was sent to Hart Island.

Hart Island is owned by New York City and operated by the New York Department of Corrections. The men, women, and children who are still being laid to rest on Hart Island are being buried by Rikers Island inmates. It is the largest tax-funded cemetery in the world. It is standard to bury adults three coffins deep and two coffins across. Babies and children are stacked five deep and up to twenty across. Amputated body parts are also disposed of here. They are placed in pine boxes marked "limbs" and buried in some random among the other coffins.

FYI: Scary nicknames include BIGGEST GRAVEYARD IN THE WORLD, NEW YORK CITY'S POTTER FIELD, and ISLAND OF THE DEAD.

The World's Weirdest Museums

Convalescent Hospital on Hart Island, 1877.

 The Hauntings

With more than one million people being unceremoniously buried in mass graves, it's no wonder this is one of the most haunted sites in the U.S. Most of these poor souls died alone, lonely, and homeless. Some died after suffering a long time from mental illness or physical afflictions. It seems that at least some of these spirits may not be able to rest in peace.

No official investigation has ever taken place on the island due to its strict security, so it is hard to speak with any certainty about paranormal activity. However, I feel certain that with this much tragic history and death, there is a lot of supernatural activity.

The sounds of boys screaming and crying in anguish have been reported by former hospital staff. It is believed these are the spirits of the reformatory boys who were badly tortured while here. Those that didn't die from the cruel abuse they were subjected to, probably died from the unsafe conditions. Contagious patients were put in the same ward as the boys. They were made to share personal items, such as razors and towels with the TB patients.

I cannot find an exact accounting of how many buildings still exist on the island. Including ruins, I believe there are at least three dozen structures. It is well- documented that there was a large hospital complex, reformatory school, and outbuildings, missile base, amusement park, and jail.

The World's Weirdest Museums

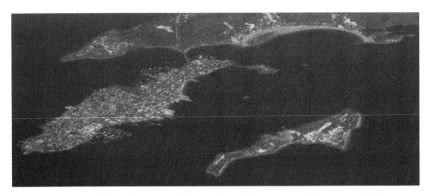

Hart Island is the smallest land mass pictured (lower right). It is accessible only by boat.

Image courtesy of Google Maps

Visitor Information

Hart Island is on the western end of Long Island Sound, next to the Bronx. No one is permitted on the one-mile-long by one-quarter-mile-wide island, except Rikers Island inmates, guards, and the deceased.

Trespassers will be prosecuted. The government is quite serious about their NO TRESPASSING policy. The only way one could get on the island is by private boat, but security is vigilant. A government ferry brings the prisoners over to the island.

To learn more about Hart Island visit https://www.hartisland.net/.

New York City is 7 hours from Cleveland, Ohio (461 miles); 12 hours from Augusta, GA (777 miles); and 4 hours from Boston, MA (214 miles).

The World's Weirdest Museums

INDEX

Amsterdam, 115, 117, 161, 164, 182
Andrea Ludden, 38
Austria, 100
Austro-Hungarian Empire, 98

Bangkok, 52, 54, 55, 159, 160
Barcelona, 83, 164
Beijing, 169
Bestattung Wien, 98
Bindeshwar Pathak, 103
Boston, 32
Brian Radam, 120
British Lawn Mower Racing Association, 122
British Museum, 170
Buddha, 174

California, 87, 147, 149, 151
Cancun, 5, 11, 12, 13, 14, 15
Cappadocia, 129
Catman2 Shelter. *See*
Chez Galip, 129
China, 169
CIA Museum, 67
Cincinnati, 126
Civil War, 4
Collection of Funeral Carriages and Hearses, 83
Congdon Anatomical Museum, 54
Croatia, 150

Dodge City, 144

Edwin Beard Budding, 123
Egypt, 61, 80

Ellis Pathological
  Museum, 54
England, 73, 165, 168,
  170, 171, 172
Eugene Belgrand, 19
Europe, 39, 97, 107,
  117, 150, 166

Florida, 48
Forbidden City, 170
France, 17, 22, 73, 89,
  169
French Quarter, 86

Galerie Hugues Aubriot,
  19
Gatlinburg, 36, 38, 40,
  49, 51
Great Britain, 119, 122
Greece, 171
Guanajuato, 111, 112,
  114
Guinness Book of
  World Records, 130

Harold Sims, 61

Hollywood, 90
Houston, 81

Iceland, 5, 33, 34, 36,
  105, 106, 107, 108
Idaho, 9, 72, 92, 95
Idaho Potato Museum,
  72
India, 104
International
  Brotherhood of
  Ventriloquists, 125
Italy, 172
Ivan Krug, 141

Japan, 134, 137
Jason deCaires Taylor,
  13
Jerry Reilly, 31
John Hunt, 166
Joseph Glidden, 139

Kansas, 6, 138, 139,
  140, 141, 143, 144,
  145, 146

The World's Weirdest Museums

Kansas Barbed Wire Collectors Association, 140
Kentucky, 124, 126

Leeds Castle, 166
London, 170, 171, 172
Loren Coleman, 43
Los Angeles, 149
Louisiana, 86
Louve, 169

Maine, 44
Massachussetts, 32
Metropolitan Museum of Art, 171
Mexican War of Independence, 115
Mexico, 11, 111, 114
Middle Ages, 117
MOBA. *See* Museum of Bad Art
Momofuku Ando, 132
MUSA, 10, 12, 15
Musée des Égouts de Paris, 19

Museo Subacuático de Arte. *See* MUSA

National Cryptologic Museum, 68
National Gallery, 171
National Gallery of Art, 173
National Museum of Korea, 173
National Palace Museum, 173
National UFO Conference, 157
National Zoological Park, 174
New Delhi, 104
New Mexico, 154, 156
New Orleans, 86, 90
New York, 108, 110, 171, 192, 197
North Carolina, 60, 61

Ohio, 126
Osaka, 134
Ottoman Empire, 171

Palace Museum, 169
Parasitology Museum, 54
Paris, 5, 9, 10, 17, 19, 20, 21, 22, 23, 24, 26, 27, 169
Paris Municipal Ossuary, 24
Pennsylvania, 77
Peter the Great, 58
Peter the Great Museum of Anthropology and Ethnography. *See* Kunstkamera
Philadelphia, 77
Portland, 44
Presidential Libraries, 68

Reykjavík, 36
Ringling Brothers Circus Museum, 48
Roswell, 156
Roswell Crash, 155
Russia, 57, 58, 59

Saint-Petersburg.
Santa Paula Cemetery, 113
Sarasota, 48
Satoru Kamegai, 136
Seoul, 173
Sigurður Hjartarson, 35
Smithsonian, 174
Songkran Niyomsane Forensic Medicine Museum, 55
South Korea, 173
Spain, 83, 164
Sulabh Sanitation Movement, 103

Taipei, 173
Taiwan, 173
Tate Modern, 172
Tennessee, 36, 38, 40, 49, 177
Texas, 81, 144
Thailand, 52, 54, 55, 158, 159, 160
Tokyo, 137
Turkey, 130

The World's Weirdest Museums

UNESCO World
　Heritage Site, 115
United States
　Lawnmower Racing
　Association, 122

Vatican Museums, 172
Vienna, 100

Village of Leeds, 168

Washington, DC, 64,
　66, 173, 174, 177
William Shakespeare
　"W.S." Berger, 125
Wisconsin, 48

Zagreb, 150

Made in the USA
Middletown, DE
27 November 2022

16170543R00110